World in Focus
India

ALI BROWNLIE BOJANG and NICOLA BARBER

WAYLAND

First published in 2006 by Wayland,
an imprint of Hachette Children's Books

This paperback edition published in 2009 by Wayland, an imprint of
Hachette Children's Books, 338 Euston Road, London NW1 3BH.
www.hachettelivre.co.uk

Commissioning editor: Victoria Brooker
Editor: Nicola Barber
Inside design: Chris Halls, www.mindseyedesign.co.uk
Cover design: Wayland
Series concept and project management by EASI-Educational Resourcing
(info@easi-er.co.uk)
Statistical research: Anna Bowden
Maps and graphs: Martin Darlison, Encompass Graphics

British Library Cataloguing in Publication Data
Brownlie Bojang, Ali, 1949
  India. - (World in focus)
  1.India - Juvenile literature
  I.Title II. Barber, Nicola
  954'.053

ISBN: 978 0 7502 4699 6

Printed and bound in China

Cover top: women at work in a factory in Bangalore.
Cover bottom: a tea plantation in Kerala, southern India.
Title page: Rajasthani women wearing traditional dress at the Pushkar Festival, Rajasthan.

Picture acknowledgements. The author and publisher would like to thank the
following for allowing their pictures to be reproduced in this publication:
Chris Fairclough Worldwide/ Chris Fairclough *cover top* 4, 31, 40, 41, 42, 53, 57, 58, 59; Corbis 5 (top) (David Samuel Robbins), 8 (Paul Almasy), 9
(Reuters/Fayaz Kabali), 10 (Stapleton Collection/ Duncan Smith), 11 (Bettmann), 12 (Reuters/ Kamal Kishore), 13 (Bettman), 16 (Reuters/ Punit Paranjpe), 18
(Lindsay Hebberd), 19 (Eye Ubiquitous/ David Cumming), 22 (Reuters/ Sunil Malhotra), 23 (Reuters/ Fayaz Kabali), 24 (Reuters/ B Mathur), 25 (Reuters/ B
Mathur), 27 Reuters/ Kamal Kishore, 28 (Pallava Bagla), 35 (Reuters/ Stringer Image), 36 (Reuters/ Amit Bhargava), 37 (Reuters/ Jagadeesh Nv), 44 (Reuters/
Ramin Talaie), 45 (Jeffrey L. Rotman), 47 (Gian Berto Vanni/Corbis), 48 (Reuters/ Raj Patidar), 49 (left) (Michael Freeman/Corbis), 49 (right) (Reuters/
Sucheta Das), 54 (Gallo Images/ Martin Harvey), 55 (Jeremy Horner); EASI-Images Rob Bowden *cover bottom*, *title page*, 5 (bottom), 6, 14, 15 (Miguel Hunt),
17, 20, 21, 26, 29, 30, 32, 33 (top and bottom), 34, 38, 39, 43, 46, 50, 51, 52, 56.

The directional arrow portrayed on the map on page 7 provides only an
approximation of north.

The data used to produce the graphics and data panels in this title were
the latest available at the time of production.

CONTENTS

CHAPTER 1

India – An Overview

Modern India is a large and exciting country full of contrasts. It has magnificent buildings, such as the massive Agra Fort, and grim, crowded urban slums. Alongside its prosperous middle class, large numbers of its population live in great poverty. It is a country that prides itself on a tradition of peaceful co-existence between people of different communities, but it has suffered violent religious clashes between Hindus and Muslims. At over 1 billion, its population is second in size only to China's, but, with a faster growth rate, India's population is set to overtake China's by the year 2030.

India has a long and rich history marked by invasions and occupations. It has experienced times of great wealth and prosperity and has been the birthplace of advancements in philosophical thinking and science – a tradition that continues today in the emerging and vibrant software industry that is helping to drive India's thriving economy (see page 31).

▼ Agra Fort, in Uttar Pradesh, was built during the reign of the Mughal emperor Akbar (see page 10) as a fortress, and partially converted into a palace by his grandson Shah Jahan (reigned 1628-58).

▲ An Indian woman shops for clothing at an outdoor stall in Varanasi, Uttar Pradesh.

India is a country with abundant natural resources, particularly coal and fertile land, and is rapidly emerging as a major economic and political power. Its rate of economic growth exceeds that of most other countries, except China, and is faster than the United Kingdom and other European countries, and the United States. Yet while economic prosperity has benefited a large and expanding middle class, these people represent only a minority of the population. There is still a huge contrast between affluent, urbanized Indians and the millions of people who strive to make ends meet on a daily basis. Poverty, particularly in the countryside, remains widespread. In many cities, slums provide a startling contrast to slick, new, high-rise office buildings and hotels. Despite its booming economy, India still ranks as one of the world's poorest nations.

Many practices and traditions that have been carried out for centuries continue to this day, particularly in the countryside. For example, subsistence farming continues largely unchanged and farmers still use oxen to plough the land. However, in many places these small farms sit alongside modern farms that use the latest technology to grow scientifically produced, hybrid varieties of crops such as cotton, rice and wheat.

The legacy of India's colonial history under the British is still apparent in its parliamentary system – India is the world's largest democracy – its judicial system, and in the use of the English language in commerce, business and politics. Another legacy of its colonial history is the ongoing conflict, created in 1947 when India gained its independence from Britain, between India and Pakistan over the disputed northern territory of Kashmir. This conflict has brought the two nations to war and, more recently, to the brink of all-out nuclear war.

▲ Many Indians live in extreme poverty. These basic shelters are home to recently arrived families in Mumbai.

◀ India is at the forefront of the computer software industry, yet oxen are still used to plough farmland across much of the country. India is full of such contrasts between the old and the new.

Culturally and historically India is very rich. It is the birthplace of two important world religions – Hinduism and Buddhism. The caste system, whereby a person's place in society is determined at birth, is still widespread in India although it contravenes the Indian constitution, which rules against discrimination (see page 25). Yet, despite the fact that India is made up of different groups of people who have been assimilated over thousands of years from different ethnic backgrounds and different religions, speaking many different languages, Indians still have a sense of belonging to one nation.

 Did you know?

India is named after the Indus river. Today, the region through which the river mainly runs is Pakistan, but it was previously part of India.

▶ The wheel indicates the Dharma Chakra, a Buddhist symbol dating back to 200 BC. The saffron colour stands for courage, sacrifice and the spirit of renunciation; the white for purity and truth; the green for faith and fertility. Saffron is also associated with Hinduism and green with Islam, the two major religions in India.

Physical geography

- Land area: 2,973,190 sq km/ 1,147,949 sq mls
- Water area: 314,400 sq km/121,390 sq mls
- Total area: 3,287,590 sq km/1,269,338 sq mls
- World rank (by area): 7
- Land boundaries: 14,103 km/8,758 mls
- Border countries: Bangladesh, Bhutan, Myanmar (Burma), China, Nepal, Pakistan
- Coastline: 7,000 km/4,347 miles
- Highest point: Kanchenjunga (8,598 m/ 28,209 ft)
- Lowest point: Indian Ocean (0 m/0 ft)

Source: CIA World Factbook

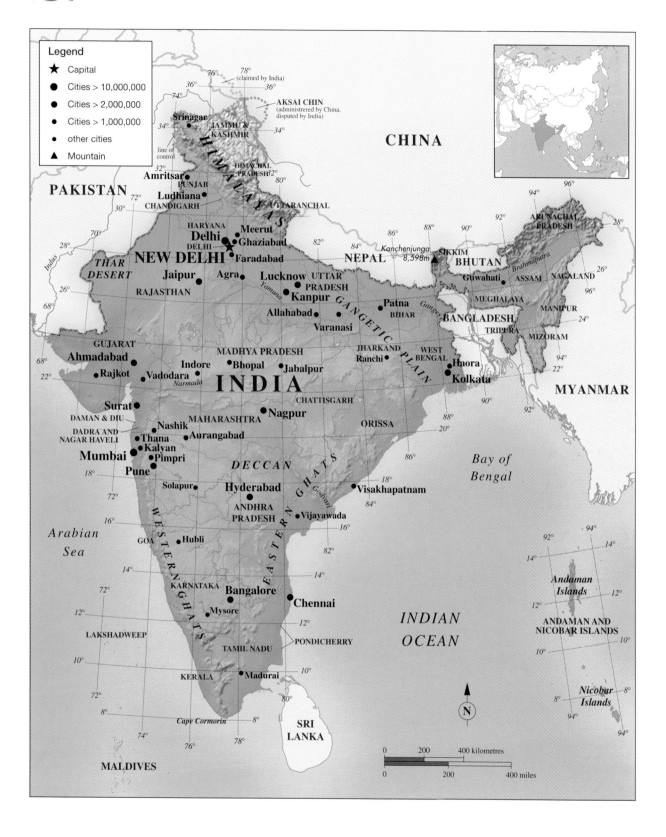

Legend
- ★ Capital
- ● Cities > 10,000,000
- ● Cities > 2,000,000
- • Cities > 1,000,000
- · other cities
- ▲ Mountain

CHAPTER 2

History

India has one of the oldest and richest civilizations in the world, dating back over 5,000 years. However, for much of its history the area we know today as India was made up of many different kingdoms and states. At times, these small states were united by dominant groups to create powerful empires, such as the Mauryan, Gupta and Mughal empires.

THE INDUS CIVILIZATION

The earliest, large-scale settlements in India's history started around 3500 BC in the fertile valley of the Indus river in the northwest – an area that is now part of modern-day Pakistan. The civilization of the Indus Valley people was based on agriculture and trade. The main urban centres were Harappa and Mohenjo-Daro, and, like other large towns built by the Indus Valley people, they were carefully planned with broad streets and sophisticated systems for water supply and drainage.

From inscriptions found on clay tablets in the Indus valley, archaeologists know that the people of the Indus civilization had developed ways of counting and measuring and that they had a written language. The Indus Valley civilization reached its peak in about 2500 BC but began to decline around 1700 BC, possibly because of natural disasters such as earthquakes and flooding.

 Did you know?

At its height, the Indus civilization extended over 1.25 million sq km (half a million sq miles) across the Indus river valley and far beyond – as far south as Mumbai, as far east as Delhi, as far west as the Iranian border and as far north as the Himalayas.

▼ The ruins of Mohenjo-Daro, once the largest city of the Indus Valley civilization.

◀ A Buddhist monk prays at a monastery in Leh, which lies high in the mountains in the northern Indian state of Jammu and Kashmir.

HINDUISM AND BUDDHISM

From around 1500 BC, a group of people called the Aryans from central Asia began to invade India. As they moved south, they established control over much of northern India, building their capital at Delhi. Their arrival pushed most of the local inhabitants, known as Dravidians, into southern India. The Aryans had their own language, Sanskrit, in which they wrote their religious texts, known as the *Vedas*. These texts are the holy books for the Hindu religion (see page 48) which developed and took a strong hold in India. In the 500s BC, another religion, Buddhism, was founded in ancient India by a man called Siddhartha Gautama who became known as the Buddha, 'the enlightened one'.

THE MAURYAN AND GUPTA EMPIRES

Other invaders into India included the Persians (from what is now Iran), who arrived in 530 BC, and the Greeks under the leadership of Alexander the Great in 326 BC. In 321 BC, a local ruler called Chandragupta Maurya took advantage of the instability caused by the Greek attacks to found an empire which, during the reign of his grandson Asoka (272-232 BC), covered much of modern-day India.

During his reign, Asoka converted to Buddhism and encouraged the spread of the religion across his vast empire. But after his death the Mauryan Empire declined and fragmented. It wasn't until the rise of the Hindu Gupta dynasty in the AD 300s, founded by Chandragupta I, that the various kingdoms and states of much of India came together once again. The Gupta Empire, which lasted until about AD 500, was a time of great advances in both the arts and the sciences, with the development of Indian classical music and dance, and the invention by Gupta mathematicians of the decimal system, and of the Hindu-Arabic numerals that we still use today.

THE MUGHAL EMPIRE

The first Muslim invaders into India were Arabs who arrived as early as the AD 700s. They were followed by successive waves of invaders from Central Asia including the Afghans and the Turks. The Muslim conquest of India began in earnest in 1192 when Muslim armies conquered much of northern India and established an empire known as the Delhi Sultanate. The Sultanate went into decline after the sack of Delhi by the ferocious Mongol leader, Timur, in 1398. A descendant of Timur, Babur, founded the Mughal Empire in 1526 – a great Muslim empire that, at its peak under Emperor Akbar (reigned 1556-1605), covered almost the whole of the subcontinent. The Mughal Empire eventually crumbled at the beginning of the eighteenth century after a series of internal revolts. However, it was the British who deposed the last Mughal emperor in 1858.

EUROPEANS IN INDIA

From the late 1400s, merchants and traders from Portugal sailed to Goa on India's west coast to trade for spices such as black pepper, cinnamon and cloves. During the 1600s, British and Dutch, and later French, traders challenged the Portuguese for this lucrative spice trade. With the permission of the Mughal emperors, the British East India Company set up various trading posts in India. During the eighteenth century, French traders became very successful in India, but after a series of battles between the two European powers Britain emerged victorious. However, in order to protect its interests, Britain had entered into numerous agreements with local rulers and gradually its commercial interests became more political. The British East India Company expanded its power across much of India until the uprising of 1857, when Indian soldiers undertook a year-long rebellion against British control. After this, in 1858, the British government took over the administration of the colony, and in 1877 Queen Victoria was proclaimed Empress of India.

◄ This exquisite miniature painting shows the Mughal emperor Akbar on a tiger hunt. It comes from the *Akbarnama*, a history of Akbar's reign written during his lifetime.

THE MOVEMENT FOR SELF-RULE

Indian resistance to British rule led a group of well-educated Indians to found the Indian National Congress Party in 1885, and as the twentieth century dawned there were increasing movements for self-rule. During World War I, more than one million Indian soldiers fought in the British army, and after the war most Indians expected an increase in self-rule in return. Instead, in 1919, British troops opened fire on a protest meeting in Amritsar, killing more than 400 people. In the aftermath of this massacre, and to support the independence movement, Mahatma Gandhi (see box) started his campaign of non-violent disobedience against the British colonizers, encouraging people to boycott British goods and to disobey laws that were considered to be discriminatory.

The British had long exploited the tensions between Hindus and Muslims in India to control the colony, and the struggle for independence only increased these tensions. The prospect of a Hindu-dominated government – the majority of the population were Hindus – troubled many Muslims. These tensions often erupted in extreme forms of violence as Muslims and Hindus alike blew up trains and carried out massacres against each other.

Focus on: Mohandas Karamchand Gandhi (1869-1948)

Mohandas Karamchand Gandhi studied law in Britain before living in South Africa where he fought for the rights of Indian workers. He returned to India in 1914 where he became known as Mahatma, 'Great Soul'. He always advocated using non-violence and passive resistance as ways of achieving political goals. One of the most famous examples of his methods was the Salt March of 1930. Salt was a basic necessity for everyone, but the British government both controlled the production and taxed the sale of salt. To draw attention to this, Gandhi and his followers walked 240 km (150 miles) to the coast where they picked up lumps of natural salt – an illegal act under the British law. The British were unsure about how to deal with Gandhi, and often imprisoned him and his followers.

▲ Mahatma Gandhi (left) on the Salt March in 1930.

HISTORY'S BIGGEST MIGRATION

India finally won its independence on 15 August 1947. During the negotiations for independence, the Muslims, led by Mohammed Ali Jinnah, argued for a separate Islamic state. Despite the opposition of Gandhi, who believed that India should not be split up, increasing violence between Hindus and Muslims convinced the British viceroy (governor) of India, Lord Mountbatten, that Partition – the term given to dividing India into separate parts – was necessary. So the subcontinent was divided into the secular nation of India and the smaller Muslim nation of Pakistan which was made up of two separate land areas on different sides of India. Then known as West Pakistan and East Pakistan, these two areas are now themselves two separate nations – Pakistan and Bangladesh. The plans for Partition were rushed through by the British causing millions of Muslims, caught on the Indian side of the border, and millions of Hindus, stranded on the Pakistani side of the border, to flee in opposite directions. Law and order broke down completely and it is estimated that in only a few weeks half a million people died, some through violence, others through starvation and the hardships they encountered. In 1948, Gandhi was himself assassinated by a Hindu fanatic who believed that he was too tolerant of Muslims.

KASHMIR AND PAKISTAN

Jawaharlal Nehru, India's first Prime Minister had a vision of socialist India, and advocated government control of important industries. He drew up economic plans to boost India's agricultural and industrial output, and adopted a policy of neutrality in foreign affairs. His rule was relatively peaceful but he was succeeded by Lal Bahadur Shastri who led two wars against Pakistan over Kashmir. The borders of this region in the north of the country had not been finalized at the time of Partition, and India and Pakistan have disputed the area ever since.

In 1971, the government of Pakistan sent forces into East Pakistan to suppress discontent over inequalities between the wealthier region in the west and the poorer, more isolated region in the east. The conflict between Pakistan and its distant eastern region sent millions of refugees into India from East Pakistan. India intervened and quickly defeated the Pakistani army. As a result of this war, East Pakistan broke away from Pakistan and became a separate Muslim nation, Bangladesh.

◀ Indian children dressed in the colours of the Indian national flag take part in a rehearsal for Independence Day celebrations in New Delhi, August 2004.

INDIRA GANDHI

After the death of Lal Bahadur Shastri, Nehru's daughter Indira Gandhi became prime minister (she was no relation of Mahatma Gandhi). During her two periods in office (1966–77 and 1980–84) there was considerable unrest. Her opponents objected to her dictatorial style of leadership and indeed she often abused her power by trying to suppress the media when they criticized her. When the opposition actually threatened her power she called a state of emergency (in 1975) and some 100,000 people were jailed without trial. In 1984, Indira Gandhi came into confrontation with followers of the Sikh religion, who were demanding a separate Sikh state within India. When Sikh militants occupied the Golden Temple at Amritsar, a holy shrine for Sikhs, Gandhi sent in government troops. Several hundred people were killed and the shrine was badly damaged. As a direct result of this action, Gandhi was assassinated in October 1984 by two of her Sikh bodyguards.

ECONOMIC BOOM

In the early 1990s India changed its political and economic policies. It followed the path taken earlier by China and opened up its markets to countries overseas and allowed private and foreign capital to be invested in the country. It built on its huge resource of well-educated but cheap labour to attract businesses to India. This strategy began the economic success that India is enjoying at the beginning of the twenty-first century. However, tensions between Hindus and Muslims have continued to trouble the country and the situation between India and Pakistan over Kashmir has worsened, representing a major challenge for both countries for the future.

▼ Prime Minister Indira Gandhi addresses a crowd in New Delhi as part of her campaign for re-election in the general election of March 1971.

CHAPTER 3

Landscape and Climate

I ndia claims to cover an area of 3,287,590 sq km (1,269,338 sq miles) (parts of this area are disputed) – slightly more than one-third of the size of the United States. It extends for 3,200 km (2,000 miles) in length from the Himalayan Mountains in the north to its southern tip, where India is separated from the independent island country of Sri Lanka by the Palk Strait.

LANDSCAPE

India is often referred to as a 'subcontinent' because it lies to the south of the great landmass of Central Asia where it forms a triangular peninsula. Physically it is bounded to the north by the Himalayan Mountains. The Arabian Sea lies to the west, the Bay of Bengal to the east and the Indian Ocean wraps around its southern coasts.

The northern region includes the sandy, dry Thar Desert in the northwest, and the huge expanse of the Gangetic Plain immediately to the south of the Himalayan Mountains, named for the Ganges river that flows through it. The Himalayas extend for 2,400 km (1,500 miles) along the northern and eastern borders of India.

Did you know?

India occupies only 2.4 per cent of the world's land area, but has approximately 17 per cent of the world's population.

▼ Rajasthan, in the northwest of India, is known as the 'desert state' because of its arid lands – including the Thar Desert. Camels are widely used for transporting goods in this region.

The second highest mountain in the world (after Everest) is K2 (8,611 m; 28,251 feet), and it lies partly within India. The highest point completely within India, Kanchenjunga (8,598 m, 28,208 feet), is also found in the Himalayan Mountains.

The Himalayan Mountains have been created by the collision of two of the plates that make up the Earth's surface. This plate boundary is also the reason why the region experiences earthquakes and landslides, for example the massive earthquake that hit the western state of Gujarat in 2001, leaving more than 30,000 people dead, and the earthquake that devastated much of Kashmir in 2005.

South of the Gangetic Plain lies a massive, triangular upland region known as the Deccan Plateau. This plateau extends to the southern tip of India at Cape Comorin and is flanked by low mountain ranges called the Eastern and Western Ghats, with average heights around 1,200 m (3,937 feet).

INDIA'S RIVERS

India is home to several large rivers, the most famous being the Ganges. Twenty-five per cent of India's land area is included in its river basin. The Brahmaputra river in the far east has the greatest volume of water because it receives higher rainfall. Both these rivers rise in the Himalayan Mountains and carry rich, fertile alluvial soils to the Gangetic Plain, providing India with its most productive farmland and irrigating vast expanses of rice and cotton fields.

>
> **Did you know?**
>
> K2 is so remote that it had no name until it was surveyed in 1856. The British surveyor T.G. Montgomery called it K2; 'K' standing for Karakoram the mountain range in which it lies, '2' meaning that it was the second peak he saw and listed. Today, K2 is the only major mountain in the world that is still known by the name given to it by its surveyor, rather than a common or local name.

▼ The Ganges is the holiest of all rivers for Hindus, and every year millions make their pilgrimage to the river at Varanasi to bathe and wash away their sins.

INDIA'S CLIMATE

Most of India has three seasons; a cool season from October to February, a hot season from March through to June and then a wet season (see page 17). However, in the south of the country, temperatures are more consistently warm or hot, even during the cool season, while the north has greater variation. For example, Chennai in the southeast has average temperatures that range from 24°C (75°F) in January to 32°C (90°F) in May and June. But during the hottest months of the year, temperatures rise to extremes on the Gangetic Plain, sometimes going as high as 49°C (120°F). In the mountain regions of the Himalayas, temperature is affected by altitude so that the average summer temperature is around 18°C (64°F) at 2,000 m (6,500 feet), dropping to 0°C (32°F) at 4,500 m (14,800 feet). Rainfall also varies across this huge country. In the arid Thar Desert in the northwest there is virtually no rain, while the states in the far northeast receive over 10,000 mm (390 inches) of rainfall annually. Most of the country is dependent on the monsoon winds that bring rainfall to much of the subcontinent from June to October.

Focus on: The Indian Ocean tsunami

On 26 December 2004 a tsunami hit the east and southwest coast of India, and engulfed the Andaman and Nicobar Islands in the Bay of Bengal. It resulted from the most powerful earthquake in the world in 40 years. The earthquake measured 9.0 on the Richter scale and took place beneath the sea just off the island of Sumatra in Indonesia. By the time the resulting waves hit the Indian coast they were up to 10 m (over 30 feet) high and travelling at a speed of 30 kph (18 mph). In India 10,749 people were killed, another 5,640 are missing, and nearly 7,000 people were injured. The waves penetrated up to 3 km (1.8 miles) inland, destroying buildings and roads, harbours and fishing boats in their wake.

◀ This aerial view, taken in January 2005, shows the devastation caused by the tsunami in Nagapattinam, a port 350 km (219 miles) south of the city of Madras.

THE MONSOONS

The monsoon winds are generated by the difference in air temperatures over the Asian landmass and the sea. From June to October a southwest wind blows from the Arabian Sea and from the Bay of Bengal, bringing warm, moist air and heavy rainfall to much of India. For the rest of the year the wind blows from the northeast, bringing dry air from the landmass of Central Asia.

India is dependent on the monsoon rains. A late monsoon, or even an early one, can cause problems for both agriculture and the economy. Sometimes heavy monsoon rains bring widespread and destructive flooding, such as the floods and landslides that hit Mumbai and Maharashtra region in central India in 2005, killing over 1,000 people. In urban areas drainage and sewage systems cannot cope with heavy rains and they frequently overflow, with dangerous and unhealthy consequences.

The monsoon rains decrease as the monsoon travels north, meaning that the northwest of the country is comparatively dry. However, sometimes the rains fail to extend their usual distance northwards. In 2002, for example, the western state of Rajasthan was hit by severe drought when it received only about half of its usual rainfall. Thousands of people were forced from the countryside to look for work in towns such as Jaipur, as their crops failed.

 Did you know?

The wettest place on earth is reported to be Mawsynram, in Meghalaya in the northeast of India. The average annual rainfall is nearly 12,000 mm (470 inches) – 10 times more than New York and 20 times more than London.

▲ Umbrellas provide protection from the monsoon rains in Kerala state. The monsoon rains are a lifeline to India, but in some years they can also bring misery.

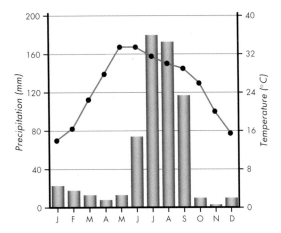

▲ Average monthly climate conditions in New Delhi

CHAPTER 4

Population and Settlements

India is the second country in the world after China to pass the 1 billion mark in terms of its population, and by 2004 India's population was estimated to be 1,147,995,898. The size of its population, and the rate at which it is growing – it more than doubled between 1960 and 2000 from 442 million to 1 billion – puts a great strain on India's resources and its capacity to ensure the health and education of all its people.

ETHNIC GROUPS

The Indian population consists of two main ethnic groups. The Indo-Aryans make up 72 per cent of the population and have their origins in the Aryan people who migrated into India about 3,500 years ago (see page 9). The Dravidians (see page 9) form 25 per cent of the population and live mainly in the south of the country. The rest of the population is made up of descendants of people who came from China and Mongolia, and tribal peoples known as Adivasis. There is also a very small number of British people and those of European origin whose families stayed in India after independence or who have settled there since.

POPULATION GROWTH

At the beginning of the twentieth century the birth-rate in India was high but it was offset by an equally high death-rate due to widespread diseases, epidemics and famines. However, from around the middle of the century the impact of improved health care, particularly mass inoculations, brought about a steady decline in the death-rate and as a consequence the rate of population growth soared.

In 1951 the government introduced family planning programmes to promote the goal of having just two children per family to slow the rate of population growth. Education about

◀ A Toda couple wear traditional *poothukulis*, the Toda native dress. The Toda are considered to be one of the earliest (Dravidian) tribes of India.

population growth became part of the school curriculum, and birth control programmes were run in hospitals and health centres throughout the country. During the Emergency in the mid-1970s (see page 13), Indira Gandhi and her son Sanjay organized a highly controversial and unpopular programme of forced sterilization for both men and women.

Although population growth has slowed down in India, many people still prefer to have a large family so that their children can contribute to the family income, and care for their parents as they get older. In particular, boy babies are highly valued and many families continue to have babies until two sons are born (see box). Many young women are married before the legal age of 18, and 49 per cent of women give birth for the first time before they reach 20. The government now recognizes the importance of more economic independence for women as one way of encouraging them to have fewer children, and it has policies in place to encourage girls to stay in school longer and marry later.

◀ A Hindu wedding in Bangalore. The wedding ceremony involves 15 different rituals and takes about three hours.

Focus on: Gender imbalance

There is evidence that the gender imbalance in India – the ratio of girls to boys – is becoming greater. In 1981 there were 962 girls per 1,000 boys under the age of six. By 2008 it was 893 per 1,000. There is a preference among many Indian families for boy babies, and modern technology has enabled many parents to know the sex of their child at a very early stage of pregnancy, sometimes resulting in a pregnancy termination if the baby is a girl. Traditionally, boys are preferred for reasons of financial security – the male is seen as the main breadwinner and therefore more likely to be able to support parents in their old age. Another factor is that parents have to pay high dowries when the time comes for their daughters to be married.

DENSITY AND DISTRIBUTION

During the twentieth century the average population density of India rose rapidly from 77 people per sq km (297 per sq mile) in 1901 to 349 per sq km (904 per sq mile) by 2008. Areas of high density are found not only in the heavily urbanized areas but also in intensively farmed rural areas, such as the fertile Gangetic Plain, where a third of India's population lives. Some border areas also have high densities because of refugees coming into India from other countries, for example near Bangladesh, Myanmar and Sri Lanka. The inaccessible, inhospitable mountainous regions of the Western and Eastern Ghats, the northeast and the Himalayas remain less populated, with densities below 110 per sq km (424 per sq mile).

CITIES, TOWNS AND VILLAGES

India has some 2,500 cities with populations exceeding 20,000 people, but most of India's population – 72 per cent – lives in more than 500,000 villages. Nearly all large Indian cities are characterized by huge building programmes and the United Nations predicts that by 2030, 50 per cent of India's population will be living in urban areas.

Population data

- Population: 1,147,995,898
- Population 0-14 yrs: 32%
- Population 15-64 yrs: 63%
- Population 65+ yrs: 5%
- Population growth rate: 1.6%
- Population density: 349.19 per sq km/ 904.40 per sq mile
- Urban population: 29%
- Major cities: Kolkata 14,787,000
  Mumbai 18,978,000
  New Delhi 15,926,000

Source: United Nations and World Bank

◀ A growing middle class in India is creating a demand for modern apartment complexes, complete with shops, restaurants, banks and schools. This development is in Mumbai.

▶ In India's cities many of the poorest people live in makeshift slums, such as this one alongside the main commuter railway line into Mumbai.

Cities in southern and central India, such as Bangalore and Hyderabad, are growing particularly rapidly as people move in from surrounding rural areas, looking to benefit from new industries such as information technology (IT). Parts of many Indian cities are now much like cities in the United States and Western Europe with shopping malls, office blocks, hotels and restaurants. However, for the poor, life in the cities is often no better than in the villages, and across India about 150 million people live in urban slums or on the streets, without adequate water supplies or waste disposal.

Village life is often in stark contrast to middle-class, urban life. Typically villages are surrounded by fields which are farmed by the villagers. Amenities can be limited, perhaps just a small shop, a primary school and a small temple or mosque. People work as farmers or carpenters, or make pots and pans, but as work becomes increasingly difficult to find, many villagers travel to local towns to look for alternative employment.

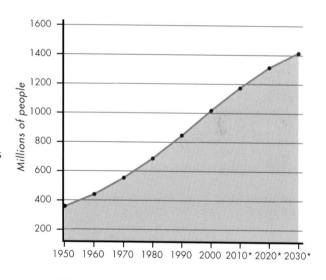

* Projected population

▲ Population growth 1950-2030

 Did you know?

The 29 per cent of India's population who live in the cities are now equivalent to the entire population of India at the time of independence in 1947.

CHAPTER 5

Government and Politics

The violence that erupted between Hindus and Muslims after Partition (see page 12) has continued to trouble India since independence in 1947. Both religious and regional differences have been the cause of serious outbreaks of unrest. For example, in 1992 widespread violence between Hindus and Muslims erupted after Hindu extremists demolished the Babri mosque at Ayodhya (see box). A decade later there was more bloodshed when Muslims attacked a train carrying Hindu pilgrims returning from Ayodhya. These events have sometimes severely threatened the democracy on which India prides itself.

Focus on: Ayodhya

Ayodhya in the northern state of Uttar Pradesh has been the focus of tension between Hindus and Muslims for many years. Many Hindus believe that it was the birthplace of Lord Rama, one of the main Hindu deities. In 1992, Hindu extremists demolished the sixteenth-century Babri mosque in Ayodhya, claiming that it stood on the site of a more ancient Hindu temple that marked the site of Rama's birth. Members of the Bharatiya Janata Party (BJP; see page 23) were involved in the destruction of the mosque, and the BJP has since backed the construction of a Hindu Rama temple on the site. A makeshift temple has been constructed, but it remains a flashpoint for religious conflict between the two communities.

▶ Hindu extremists storm the Babri mosque in Ayodhya, December 1992.

INDIAN DEMOCRACY

India has the largest democracy in the world – it has more people voting in a general election than in any other country. During the general election of 2004, for example, there were some 660 million voters. In this election, India also became the first country in the world in which everyone voted by means of an electronic voting machine. Over one million machines were needed to cover the entire country.

Indian voters have plenty of political parties from which to choose – more than 500. However, the main national parties are the Congress Party which has been predominant for most of the time since 1947, and the Bharatiya Janata Party (BJP) a Hindu nationalist party which promotes the concerns of Hindus in India. The BJP emerged as a major force in Indian politics in the 1990s, and its leader Atal Bihari Vajpayee became prime minister in 1998. In 2004 the Congress Party was voted back into power and Manmohan Singh, a Sikh (see page 49) and a former governor of India's Central Bank, became prime minister. He is the first Sikh to be appointed as the country's leader.

◀ A Kashmiri woman casts her vote on an electronic voting machine in Sheeri, 61 km (40 miles) northwest of Srinigar, in the Indian general elections of 2004. Each party has its own symbol alongside its name. The BJP's logo is a lotus flower, the logo of the Congress Party is a hand.

NATIONAL AND STATE GOVERNMENT

India is a federal republic made up of 28 states and seven union territories. The seat of Indian national government is in the capital, New Delhi. The president of India is chosen every five years by members of parliament, and is essentially a figurehead who represents India on ceremonial occasions. Political power lies with the central government, which is based on the British system with a prime minister and two houses of parliament – the upper Council of States (Rajya Sabha), and the House of the People (Lok Sabha). The Rajya Sabha has a maximum of 250 members, 12 of whom are selected by the president. The other 238 are elected by the parliaments of the 28 states and seven union territories. In the Lok Sabha up to a maximum of 550 members are directly elected by the Indian people in general elections and

two members can be appointed by the president. They serve for up to five years. The prime minister is advised by a council of ministers who are answerable to the Lok Sabha.

Each state has its own parliament, which is able to make specific laws for the state on matters such as health care, transportation and education. The state governments are headed by a chief minister and the president also appoints a governor for each state. However the national government is able to impose direct rule from New Delhi if it feels it needs to, during an emergency for example.

▼ The Indian Prime Minister, Manmohan Singh, at the European Union Business Summit in New Delhi, September 2005.

THE INDIAN CONSTITUTION

India is a secular state. This means that the government has officially remained separate from any one religion, allowing all forms of worship equal status. The Indian constitution is based on rights and democracy, and places a strong emphasis on an end to inequalities in society and social welfare, for example requiring the government to set goals for a minimum wage and subsidized health care. However, as a result of political corruption and the misuse of power there have been times when the constitution has been ineffective in protecting the rights of Indian citizens, for example during the Emergency in the 1970s, when Indira Gandhi was prime minister (see page 13).

▼ Members of the Congress Party gather inside the central hall of the Indian parliament building in New Delhi to elect the head of their party in May 2004.

Focus on: The Gandhi dynasty

The Nehru-Gandhi family has dominated Indian politics for most of its independent history. Indira Gandhi was the daughter of India's first prime minister, Jawaharlal Nehru. After her assassination in 1984 (see page 13), she was succeeded by her son Rajiv. He, too, was assassinated in 1991. His Italian-born widow, Sonia, was reluctantly drawn into politics to help the Congress Party win the general election in 2004. Although she declined the offer to become prime minister, Sonia took over the role of party president. Her children, Rahul and Priyanka, both won seats in the 2004 election and look set to continue the Gandhi dynasty.

CHAPTER 6

Energy and Resources

India is rich in natural resources, sources of energy and land suitable for cultivation despite its high population density. The rapid rate of industrialization and urbanization is creating a growing demand for energy to run new factories and supply businesses. While the majority of the population still use traditional forms of energy such as burning wood and dried cow dung for cooking and heating water, with increasing wealth comes the demand for more energy for domestic products such as fridges and fans and, for the more affluent, televisions, washing machines and personal computers.

India's per capita energy consumption rose by about 45 per cent between 1985 and 2005, compared to a rise of 5 per cent in the United States and 8 per cent in the United Kingdom (UK) in the same period. This is one of the highest energy consumption growth rates in the world, along with that of China. But because of its relative lack of development compared to other countries, India's per capita energy use is still only about 6 per cent of that of the United States, and 13 per cent of that of the UK. Pressure will increase as India's demand for energy grows at an expected annual rate of 4.6 per cent through to the year 2010.

ENERGY PRODUCTION

Most of India's electricity is generated from burning coal, of which it has large reserves mainly in Madhya Pradesh, Bihar and West Bengal. It is estimated that these reserves, the fourth largest in the world after the United States, Russia and China, will last until 2233. India also has reserves of oil and gas offshore from Mumbai, and in Assam and Gujarat.

◄ Energy consumption per person in India is low, but it is rising fast as the demand for consumer electronics increases.

Another source of electricity, growing in importance, is energy from hydroelectric power (HEP). About 50 per cent of HEP is produced by reservoirs high up in the Himalayas, while over 4,000 large dams have been built across major rivers elsewhere to provide plants to produce the rest. The increase in demand for energy for both industrial and domestic use has put pressure on India's energy sources and has led to some controversial plans for supplying energy, such as the Narmada river dams (see box).

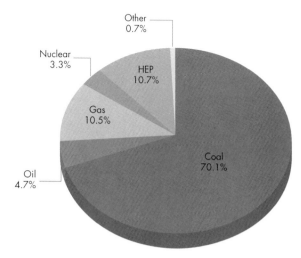

▲ Electricity production by type

Focus on: The Narmada dams

The construction of large dams on the Narmada river has become one of the most important social issues in India, drawing attention from campaigners all around the world. In 2000, as part of a major campaign against these dams, thousands of people marched and demonstrated in protest against the Indian government. The subsequent flooding of the valley behind the largest of the dams, the Sardar Sarovar dam, deprived up to one million people, mostly poor farmers, of their homes and their land. However, in March 2005 the Supreme Court of India ruled that those displaced must receive adequate compensation.

► Demonstrators in New Delhi in November 2000 protest against the construction of the Sardar Sarovar dam.

Energy data

- Energy consumption as % of world total: 5%
- Energy consumption by sector (% of total):
  Industry: 27.1%
  Transportation: 12.3%
  Agriculture: 2.7%
  Services: 0.8%
  Residential: 55.6%
  Other: 1.5%
- CO_2 emissions as % of world total: 3.9%
- CO_2 emissions per capita in tonnes p.a.: 0.9

Source: World Resources Institute

India has plans to increase the proportion of electricity that comes from nuclear energy – just 3.3 per cent of power production in 2005 – and has eight nuclear reactors under construction. India also has one the largest national programmes to promote the use of solar power. In many villages this is not only more environmentally friendly than many other forms of producing electricity, it is more cost-effective as well.

MINERAL RESOURCES

As well as its large reserves of coal, India's rich abundance of mineral resources includes iron ore, manganese, bauxite, diamonds and limestone, as well as other valuable minerals.

India is one of the most important producers of iron ore in the world. Two-thirds of India's iron ore reserves are in the states of Orissa and Bihar. There is a global demand for iron ore to produce steel, especially from China. India also exports iron ore to Japan, Iran and Taiwan. After Russia, India has the largest supply of manganese and other economically useful minerals such as bauxite and copper. Diamonds and other gems are also an important resource,

providing a valuable part of India's export industry. In Jaipur, Rajasthan, local gem stones supply a thriving jewellery industry.

LAND AND AGRICULTURE

Over half of India's land area is suitable for cultivation, providing a particularly valuable resource. Rice is the most widely grown crop, and it provides the staple food for 65 per cent of the Indian population. The main rice-growing areas are in the south and the east. Rice is also cultivated on the fertile Gangetic Plain along with wheat, which is a staple food in northern India. The Deccan Plateau also has fertile black soils which are particularly good for growing cotton.

Indian cotton is the basis of the textile and clothing industry in India. Cotton accounts for 30 per cent of India's agricultural gross domestic product. India's 4 million cotton farmers plant more land with cotton than anywhere else in the world and produce 12 per cent of the world's cotton. But yields per

▲ A worker picks lint from cotton plants. These genetically modified plants are being field tested under controlled conditions in India.

acre are comparatively low and many farmers are interested in genetically modified strains of cotton that could improve yields. Some think this 'gene revolution' could be India's new Green Revolution (see box).

India is the world's largest tea producer and in 2005 had nearly 40,000 tea estates employing a workforce of over 2 million. However, in recent years India has faced increasing competition from Sri Lanka and Kenya as well as a general slump in global demand for tea. India is second only to Brazil in the production of sugar cane, and is the largest consumer of sugar in the world.

Woodlands cover 22 per cent of India's land area. The trees range from deciduous woodlands in the temperate northern districts to dense, tropical forests in the Western Ghats. Teak, rosewood and sal are grown commercially for furniture, while bamboo is used as scaffolding in the building industry. However, deforestation is a major problem across the country (see page 56).

Focus on: The 'Green Revolution'

From 1967 to the late 1970s, the so-called 'Green Revolution' changed India from an importer to an exporter of food. Following a number of failed monsoons in the 1960s, and its resulting dependency on the United States for food aid, India introduced new methods of agriculture to achieve self-sufficiency in food. The area of land used for agriculture was expanded, two crops a year were grown instead of one, and new strains of high-yield seeds, mainly wheat and rice, were introduced. The results were record grain crops in the late 1970s. But the new methods required increased use of fertilizers and pesticides which can cause environmental problems, as well as improved irrigation which led to the construction of many dams.

▼ The current building boom in India is creating an enormous demand for timber to be used for scaffolding and for shuttering for concrete.

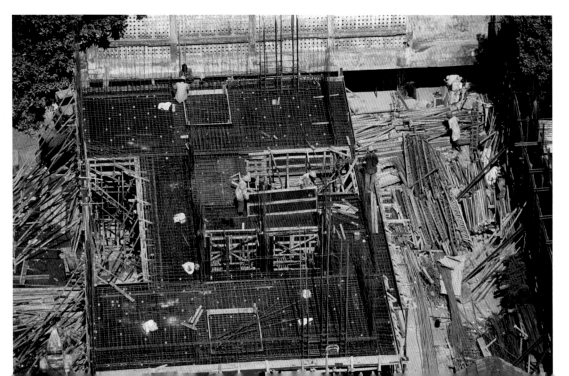

CHAPTER 7

Economy and Income

At independence India's economy was dominated by traditional agriculture and cash crops such as tea, sugar and cotton. At the beginning of the twenty-first century its economy still encompasses traditional village farming, but commercial agriculture, handicrafts, modern industry and a multitude of service industries – particularly information technology (IT) – now play an increasingly dominant role.

ECONOMIC CHANGE

Before the 1990s, the Indian government exercised strict control over the economy, imposing high taxes on imports from abroad and limiting foreign involvement. This government control had the effect of protecting Indian industries and businesses from foreign competition, but by the 1980s it was clear that this system was stifling development, as Indian companies fell behind their international counterparts. From 1991, the government opened up the Indian economy to the outside world, allowing foreign investment, competition and trade.

The government has set up free-trade zones, such as the Madras Export Processing Free Trade Zone, where foreign companies can invest without having to pay duties and taxes,

▲ Tea remains one of India's most important agricultural exports. This large estate in Kerala, southern India, is owned by Tata Tea.

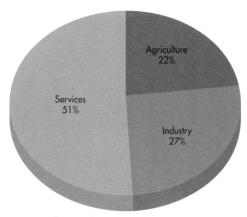

▲ Economy by sector

Economic data

- Gross National Income (GNI) in US$: 1,069,427,000
- World rank by GNI: 12
- GNI per capita in US$: 950
- World rank by GNI per capita: 160
- Economic growth: 9.2%

Source: World Bank

making it easier for manufacturing industries to develop. For example, sales of cars made in India increased between 2002 and 2003 by a huge 41 per cent. In 2007 India was ranked among the top 12 industrial nations with its gross domestic product (GDP) estimated to be worth over US$1 trillion and to be growing at a rate of more than 9 per cent in that year.

INFORMATION TECHNOLOGY

A crucial factor in boosting India's economy has been its role as a front-runner in the fields of IT, biotechnology and communications. In 1998 software and related IT services contributed about 1.2 per cent to India's GDP, by 2008 this sector had grown to account for about 5.5 per cent of GDP. This growth is expected to continue as increasing numbers of overseas companies move their software work 'offshore' to India to benefit from India's low-cost engineers. Many companies in the UK and the United States have outsourced some parts of

their operations to India, particularly call centres (see page 37), because they can pay far less in wages to employees in India than in their home countries. There are over 40 software parks located around major cities such as Bangalore, Chennai, Mumbai, Puna and Hyderabad.

AGRICULTURE

Despite all these changes in India's economy, agriculture remains an important factor in the country's economy. Sixty per cent of India's workforce is employed in the agriculture sector, and agriculture still constitutes 22 per cent of India's GDP.

 Did you know?

India is the world's third largest producer of satellites, and its INSAT system is one of the world's biggest domestic satellite communication systems.

▼ Women in a factory in Bangalore, Karnataka, work at wiring circuit boards for TV production.

Focus on: Bangalore

The southern city of Bangalore, the capital of the state of Karnataka, was once known as a retreat for older people who were attracted by its temperate climate and relaxed atmosphere. But by 2005 it was the fastest growing city in Asia and had become known as the 'Silicon Valley of the East'. In 2004 there were some 1,400 IT companies based in Bangalore, many of them foreign firms set up to take advantage of the city's vast pool of computer-literate, English-speaking workers. These companies have brought a new prosperity to the city, with over 520,000 people employed in the sector in 2007. These employees are mostly young people with money to spend, and Bangalore's main shopping street – Mahatma Gandhi Road (known as MG Road) is full of designer shops, restaurants, bars and restaurants.

RISE IN CONSUMERISM: CONTINUING POVERTY

The success of the economy has led to the emergence of a powerful new group of people in Indian society, the so-called 'middle class'. The new middle class are found in urban and rural areas and include business people and wealthy farmers, professionals and white-collar workers. They are well-educated and have disposable income to purchase goods such as fashion clothes, CD and DVD players and to engage in leisure activities. In turn, the increased purchasing power of the middle class helps to boost the economy. In fact, India's own industries struggle to keep pace with people's demand for goods, and India will have to import more goods unless it can increase the rate at which its manufacturing industries are growing. But despite the growing prosperity of the middle

▼ Modern shopping malls, such as this one in Jaipur, cater for a growing consumer class in India.

◀ A shoe-mender in a makeshift street-side shelter. Such activities are typical of the informal sector.

class, it is estimated that 35 per cent of the Indian population continues to live on less than US$1 a day, and 80 per cent on less than US$2 a day. India was ranked as low as 128 out of 177 countries on the United Nation's development index in 2008, which takes into account people's quality of life, including factors such as education and health, as well as their material wealth.

THE INFORMAL SECTOR

In some of the large cities such as Delhi, Chennai and Mumbai, the informal sector of the economy accounts for around 67 per cent of total employment. This means that people are involved in menial or temporary work usually on a casual basis, and either never reach levels of income where they would pay tax, or they simply avoid paying tax. Typical jobs in this sector include street-selling, cleaning, working as security guards or domestic servants, and employment in textile workshops. Employment is frequently neither registered nor monitored and as a result the conditions in which people work are often unregulated, unhealthy and dangerous. Many of the people working in this

sector are migrants from rural areas who have few skills, and are therefore unable to get better-paid or more secure jobs.

▼ The *dhobi ghats* in Mahalakshmi, Mumbai. Every day thousands of items of laundry are processed here. It is an example of how India's seemingly chaotic informal economy can work faultlessly.

CHAPTER 8

Global Connections

India has had strong trade links with the rest of the world for many centuries. In colonial times, many Indians went as indentured labourers to far-flung parts of the British Empire – promised fair wages and a passage home in return for a fixed number of years' labour. Some of these labourers chose to stay at the end of their indenture, and vibrant communities of people of Indian origin are now part of, for example, South Africa and the Caribbean. In more recent times India has experienced a 'brain-drain', as many of its most talented people have moved to countries such as the United States (see page 43). India's influence in music, art, cuisine, dance and science can be seen all over the world.

▼ Textiles were one of the first commodities to be traded by India, and the Indian textile industry is still an important part of the country's economy. This factory is in Mumbai, India's main textile centre.

INTERNATIONAL ORGANIZATIONS

India was a founder member of the United Nations (UN). Today it works closely with the United Nations to achieve the Millennium Development Goals, a list of targets set by the UN to eradicate poverty, improve health and education, ensure sustainable development and develop global partnerships by 2015. Like many other countries that were colonized by Britain, India has been an important member of the Commonwealth since its independence.

TRADE AND INVESTMENT

India recognizes the importance of links with other countries for its future prosperity, not only in terms of trade but also in opening its doors to investment from other countries, and itself investing in foreign companies. India's largest trading partner is the United States from which it buys aircraft and parts, machinery, fertilizers and computer hardware. India's main exports are textiles and ready-made garments, agricultural products, gems and jewellery, leather products and chemicals. Its other main trading partners are China, the UK, Belgium, Hong Kong and Singapore. As a member of the World Trade Organization (WTO), India has had to simplify its tariffs for countries importing their goods into India and reduce export restrictions.

India is a leading member of two powerful country groupings, the G3 and the G20+. The G3, formed in 2003, is made up of Brazil, South

Africa and India and its purpose is to speak with one, powerful voice in negotiations with the rich, industrialized G8 countries (the United States, the UK, France, Germany, Japan, Italy, Canada and Russia). The G20+ includes Argentina, Brazil, China and South Africa, as well as India. This group of developing countries has built a common position to fight against the subsidies that are paid to farmers in the United States and the European Union (EU), and against barriers to agricultural trade. The G20+ has shown that it has a powerful voice. At a WTO meeting in Cancun, Mexico, in 2003, negotiators from G20+ pressed the EU and the United States for the phasing-out of farm subsidies so that their own markets would not be flooded by inexpensive farm imports. The talks collapsed when the two sides could not come to an agreement. Negotiations have since continued with more success.

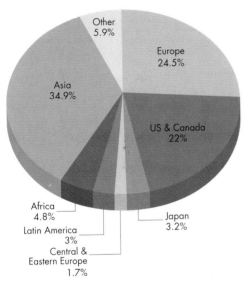

▲ Destination of exports by major trading region

▲ Indian soldiers keep guard on the 'line of control' in 2001 in the northern state of Jammu and Kashmir, near the disputed border with Pakistan.

RELATIONS WITH NEIGHBOURS

Relations between India and its neighbour Pakistan have been strained since 1947 (see page 12). After Partition, disputes quickly broke out over the state of Jammu and Kashmir (often referred to simply as Kashmir) on the border of the two countries when the Hindu ruler of this predominantly Muslim

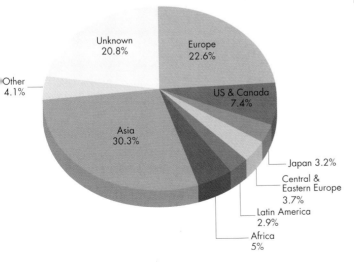

▲ Origin of imports by major trading region

state opted to become part of India. A UN ceasefire gave control of certain areas of Kashmir to each country. However, neither side has accepted a divided Kashmir as a permanent solution and there have since been two further wars leading to a real threat of nuclear war. Both India and Pakistan have nuclear weapons and in 1998 both countries carried out nuclear tests, partly as a way of intimidating each other. However, in 2004 the two countries agreed on a peace process over Kashmir, and there were hopeful signs as India withdrew some of its troops, and as bus services started across the disputed border region in Kashmir for the first time in 60 years (see page 58).

India has had disputes with its neighbours over water resources. In the 1960s, there were hostilities between India and Pakistan over India's construction of the Farakka Barrage on the Ganges river near the border between India and East Pakistan. The barrage was completed in 1970, and diverts water out of the Ganges into the Bhagirati-Hoogly River. After independence in 1971, Bangladesh continued to press the case against India, claiming that the dam deprived Bangladesh of vital water resources. Another dispute with Pakistan is over the construction by India of the Baglihar hydroelectric plant on the Indus river in Kashmir. The Baglihar dam was completed in 2007, but disputes continue over its operation, and the effect on the Indus River basin.

▶ Dr Naresh Trehan at work in an operating room in New Delhi. Dr Trehan moved to the United States in 1969 where he was a highly successful heart surgeon. He has since returned to India, prompted largely by Indian nationals who were seeking his services in the United States, and asking why they could not get the same quality of care back home.

India's relations with China slowly improved towards the end of the twentieth century after many years of tensions over borders. However, India and China now share much in common as emerging and vibrant Asian economies, and in 2005 talks took place between the two countries on how they could co-operate more closely in developing their respective software technologies and other mutual interests.

WORKING OVERSEAS

Since the 1970s, migrant Indian workers have been going to work in oil-rich Saudi Arabia. By 2004 it was estimated that there were some 3 million Indians working there. The money they send home is a vital source of income for many families, although some reports claim that many Indians in Saudi Arabia work in very poor conditions in hospitals, domestic homes and service industries such as garbage collection.

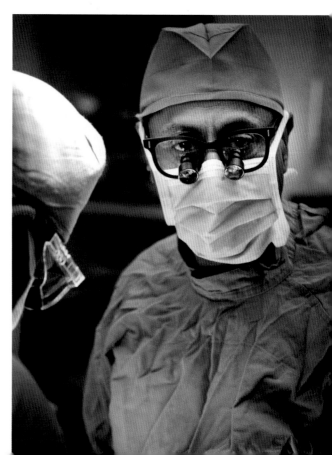

Many professional Indian men and women, particularly those working in IT and the professions, including doctors, nurses and engineers, have been actively recruited by agencies in the United States and the UK. It is estimated there are about 1.6 million Indians concentrated in California, New York, New Jersey, Illinois and Texas in the United States. According to World Bank figures, India receives more money than any other country from its migrant workers abroad – US$25.1 billion in 2006.

Focus on: Call centres

Many companies in the United States and the UK have outsourced work to call centres in India. These call centres handle a wide range of processing jobs from answering customer service calls to telesales, credit demands and accounting. Companies such as British Telecom have moved large parts of their operations to India, taking advantage of the lower wage costs. It is estimated that UK companies can make a saving of 40 per cent by outsourcing in this way. There is also the attraction of a good supply of well-educated and skilled workers in India. In 2008 outsourcing has continued, but staffing costs are rising as Indians demand higher wages, making both international and Indian companies look for other options.

▼ An Indian woman answers a call at a call centre in the southern Indian city of Bangalore.

CHAPTER 9

Transport and Communications

A good transport system is essential to the economic growth of any country and particularly one the size of India. Increased economic activity and development is putting pressure on the government to modernize and improve all transport networks.

 Did you know?

Indian Railways runs almost 14,000 trains, on 63,221 km (39,284 miles) of track covering 6,853 stations, and carries more than 15 million passengers every day. It is the largest civilian employer in the world with 16 million employees.

INDIA'S RAILWAY SYSTEM

The British began the construction of the Indian railway system in 1853, and within 50 years 37,014 km (23,000 miles) of track had been laid. The railways have expanded to become the most important mode of transport for the movement of goods and people around India. Although the trains and carriages are often built to lower standards of comfort than in the West, trains are affordable and usually

▼ People wait to wish departing relatives and friends farewell at a station. Trains are the most affordable means of long-distance travel for the majority of people in India.

efficient. However, commuter trains taking people from the suburbs to the city centres for work are often very crowded, with people crammed in, and many hanging on dangerously to the outside of the trains.

In order to ease its traffic chaos, Delhi opened a new metro system in 2003. The metro has a total length of 21.3 km (13.2 miles) of track and 18 stations. Most of the track is elevated and the carriages and stations are air-conditioned. The metro is integrated with other transport systems, such as bus and rail, to make journeys as easy and efficient as possible. Mumbai has also been investing in improvements to its suburban railways which link its rapidly expanding suburbs with the city centre.

ROAD TRANSPORT

India has the second-largest network of roads in the world, totalling 3,383,344 km (2,102,313 miles). However, only just under half of these roads are tarmac and only 4 per cent conform to internationally recognized standards. In many country areas, roads are no more than single lane paths that are impassable in heavy rains. The most important highway is the so-called Golden Quadrilateral, 5,846 km (3,633 miles) of road linking New Delhi, Mumbai, Chennai and Kolkata. The government is upgrading 10,000 km (6,200 miles) of this road by 2012 at a cost of US$6.9 billion. The World Bank is also investing US$665 million in road projects around India, for example to improve rural roads in selected areas.

There has been a staggering increase in the number of cars and other vehicles in India. Numbers have been doubling every seven years since 1970, and today there are about 70 million vehicles on India's roads. India is infamous for its cities' traffic jams in which the streets are clogged with cars, motorbikes and auto rickshaws – three-wheeled taxis with space for two passengers. In addition, the rapid increase in road traffic, poorly regulated licensing of drivers and the poor state of the roads has led to high accident rates across the country.

▶ Rush-hour traffic in Jaipur is a chaotic mix of rickshaws, motorbikes and a growing number of private cars. The same is true for other cities in India, causing major congestion and pollution problems.

AIR TRAVEL

The huge size of India and the slowness of train travel means that air travel is an attractive option for those who can afford it. New budget airlines are mushrooming in India. The boom was started in 2003 by Air Deccan, based in Bangalore, when it offered fares between Delhi and Mumbai for a price as low as 500 rupees (£11/US$20). Many airlines, such as Kingfisher Airlines, Spice Jet and Go Air are following suit to provide cheap, no-frills alternatives to the major airlines.

GETTING CONNECTED

It was estimated that in the year 2008, India had 60 million Internet users. This is up from some 25 million in 2005 – a huge and rapid increase, although still small in terms of the percentage of the total population. For the inhabitants of rural areas, getting connected to the Internet can present problems as electricity supplies are often intermittent (and in some places non-existent), and landlines for telephones often provide unreliable and slow links. New wireless technology is being piloted in some rural areas to explore alternative ways of connecting rural villages to the Internet.

Mobile phones were first introduced in India in 1994. At this time only a few privileged people could afford to use them. But prices have fallen

Focus on: High-speed links

India is one of the first countries in the world to provide high-speed Internet access from trains. By 2004, 40,000 km (24,900 miles) of fibre-optic cable had been laid around the country to provide communication links not just for trains but also for cyber-cafés in stations to serve local communities.

▼ A young man logs on to the worldwide web at an Internet café in New Dehli.

and by 2008 it was estimated that, at around 233 million users, there were nearly five times more mobile phones than fixed landlines in India. This is an increase of over two hundred million since 2003, at a rate of 3.4 million new mobile phones every month.

THE PRESS

During the time of the Emergency, under Indira Gandhi, the government tried to prevent newspapers writing articles that were critical of their policies. Today, however, the Indian press is independent and lively debates take place over important issues of the day. There are over 5,000 daily newspapers in different languages.

▲ A newspaper and magazine stand in Delhi. The major English-language papers are the most widely read and include the *Times of India, The Hindu, The Statesman, The Indian Express, India World* and *The Economic Times.*

Transport & communications data

- ▱ Total roads: 3,383,344 km/2,102,313 miles
- ▱ Total paved roads: 1,603,705 km/996,496 miles
- ▱ Total unpaved roads: 1,779,639 km/ 1,105,816 miles
- ▱ Total railways: 63,221 km/39,284 miles
- ▱ Airports: 346
- ▱ Cars per 1,000 people: 12
- ▱ Mobile phones per 1,000 people: 204
- ▱ Personal computers per 1,000 people: 28
- ▱ Internet users per 1,000 people: 52

Source: World Bank and CIA World Factbook

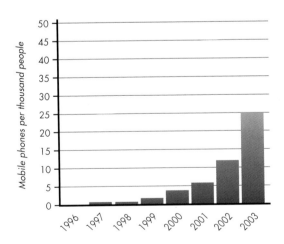

▲ Mobile phone use 1995-2003

Education and Health

Since independence India has recognized the need for its people to be well-educated and healthy if the country is to develop and progress as a nation. With 35 per cent of its population under the age of 15, India is faced with a massive task. Nevertheless, literacy rates have risen dramatically since independence, from 15 per cent in 1947 to 61 per cent in 2008.

THE EDUCATION SYSTEM

Each state in India has its own system of education, so standards vary as some states invest more in education than others. For example, the state of Kerala at the south-western tip of India has prioritized education and has the highest literacy rate in the country, at 91 per cent. Across the country, primary and middle school education from six to 14 years is free and compulsory, although parents must buy books and other equipment for their children, which is a struggle for many poor families. Secondary or high school is not free,

and parents must pay fees for tuition as well as equipment. Private schools are popular among the upper and middle classes. Many secondary school students go on to higher education at university or college.

POOR-QUALITY EDUCATION

While all children should by law go to primary and middle school, in many states the record of attendance is poor. India has nearly 600,000 primary schools, but many of these are small village schools often with dilapidated buildings and no facilities. There is a shortage of teachers in rural areas, and it is common for teachers not to turn up for classes – on average teachers in India are absent from the classroom for 25 per cent of the time. The quality of the teaching is sometimes poor, and the curriculum being taught fails to capture the interest of many pupils. In 2004 about 135 million pupils were enrolled in primary and middle schools. However, records kept from 1996-2005 show that only 79 per cent of boys and 72 per cent of girls actually attended school. The government is making great efforts to improve the quality of the curriculum that is taught in schools. It is also encouraging participation at a local level, with Village Education Committees and parent-teacher associations giving parents more direct involvement in the education of their children.

◀ Boys at a private school in Delhi play soccer in their school's playing fields.

SECONDARY AND HIGHER EDUCATION

By secondary school the number of students attending has dropped to 51 million (from 135 million), indicating that many children leave school early to work, or because their parents cannot afford to keep them there.

Many of those who succeed in secondary school go to one of India's 256 universities or 12,000 Institutes of Higher Education. Every year India produces about 3 million graduates. India's education system has traditionally placed emphasis on mathematics and the sciences, resulting in a large number of science and engineering graduates.

▶ Lessons are held outside at this rural primary school in Rajasthan. Many schools in India lack proper buildings and equipment.

Focus on: The 'brain-drain'

Indian universities produce 135,000 engineering graduates each year. The most skilled are often tempted to move overseas for better pay. Despite the fact that salaries for those working in IT in India increased over 15 per cent in 2006, these salaries still represent only a quarter of their equivalents in the United States. Many people consider this 'brain-drain' to be a huge loss of human capital and investment in education for India. Others claim that Indians learn new skills abroad and point to the large amounts of money that is sent back to India by these workers (see page 36). However, there is some evidence that the 'brain-drain' is starting to slow down as Indian's economy continues to grow, and as the domestic job market becomes increasingly attractive.

Education and health

- Life expectancy at birth male: 66.9
- Life expectancy at birth female: 71.9
- Infant mortality rate per 1,000: 32.3
- Under five mortality rate per 1,000: 76
- Physicians per 1,000 people: 0.6
- Health expenditure as % of GDP: 5.0%
- Education expenditure as % of GDP: 3.8%
- Primary net enrolment: 89%
- Pupil-teacher ratio, primary: 40
- Adult literacy as % age 15+: 61%

Source: United Nations Agencies and World Bank

▲ An official checks the finger markings of a baby girl to make sure she has received her polio drops.

DIFFERENCES IN HEALTH CARE

Standards of health care in India vary widely. In urban areas there are large hospitals boasting the latest medical technology for those who can afford to pay for treatment. But in many rural areas health care is poor, and many people live miles away from the nearest basic health facilities. Government health expenditure in 2007 was 5 per cent of GDP, but over the years it has not grown to meet the increasing demands and needs of the expanding population.

Many poor people in India suffer from diseases that are a direct result of their living conditions. Malnutrition, poor sanitation and lack of clean drinking water are the main problems, causing diseases such as typhoid and dysentery. Children who are weakened by malnutrition have little resistance to various diarrhoeal diseases, and these diseases are the main cause of childhood death. Although the infant mortality rate (the number of infants under age one dying per year) has fallen, it is still 32 per 1,000 children born – a high figure compared to the United States where it is 6 per 1,000 births, or the UK where it is 5 per 1,000. By some measures, such as immunisation rates, standards are actually falling. In 1994, for example, 91 per cent of children were vaccinated against polio and 96 per cent against tuberculosis; in 2006 these figures had dropped to 78 per cent and 58 per cent respectively. Malaria, tuberculosis and leprosy are prevalent throughout India.

As urban India adopts more Western life-styles, fast-food restaurants and more sedentary jobs are creating changes in the health of young Indians. Not surprisingly, these changes mainly affect the affluent upper and middle classes, and it is estimated that around 30 per cent of India's well-off teenagers are overweight. Changes in diet and the increase of obesity is giving cause for concern about future health problems, particularly coronary diseases.

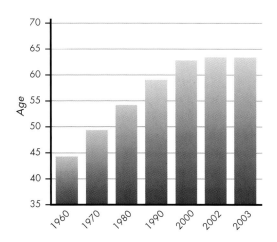

▲ Life expectancy at birth 1960-2003

HIV/AIDS

The number of people with HIV/AIDS is steadily rising in India, and this disease poses a huge potential problem for the future. It was estimated that in 2008 the number of people living with HIV/AIDS in India was more than 2 million. Its spread has been attributed mainly to prostitution, the sexual habits of some migrant workers – particularly long-distance truck drivers, the use of unsterilized needles by drug addicts, and infected blood used for transfusions. Widespread ignorance and fear of the disease is being addressed by government programmes that aim to educate people about HIV/AIDS, and encourage young people to adopt safe and responsible lifestyles. Data indicates that the epidemic is now stabilising, with fewer people becoming infected on a yearly basis.

Focus on: Medical tourism

In 2004, George Marshall, a 73-year-old violin repairer from Bradford in the UK, paid £4,800 (US$8,425) to have a heart bypass operation in a hospital in Bangalore. At home in the UK he was faced with the choice of waiting six months or paying £19,000 for the operation. In the same year, 150,000 people visited India for treatment. It is estimated that by 2012 this kind of 'medical tourism' could be worth 100 billion rupees (£1.24 billion/US$2.1 billion) to India.

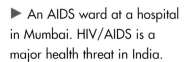

▶ An AIDS ward at a hospital in Mumbai. HIV/AIDS is a major health threat in India.

CHAPTER 11

Culture and Religion

With its historical mix of peoples from many different parts of Asia and Europe, and its population of over 1 billion people, it is impossible to speak of any one single Indian culture. There are, however, strong cultural and historical threads that have helped to develop a strong sense of nationhood amongst the Indian people.

LANGUAGES

Many different languages are spoken in India. The national language of India is Hindi, but it is the first language for only 41 per cent of Indians, most of whom live in the north. The vast majority speak one of 14 other official regional languages. Hindi is one of the family of Indo-European languages, and others in this group include Bengali, Gujarati, Punjabi and Urdu. People in the south of India speak Dravidian languages such as Kannada, Tamil, Telugu and Malayalam. English is India's second official language, and is commonly used as the language of business, commerce, politics and higher education. Most educated Indians speak several languages.

 Did you know?

In addition to the official regional languages of India there are more than 1,650 different dialects spoken.

FOOD

Not surprisingly in a country as large and diverse as India, food varies from region to region. It also varies according to culture and religion. For example, Hindus do not eat beef, and many eat no meat at all. Muslims do not eat pork. In the north of the country, the staple diet is based on meat, vegetables and bread such as *chapatis* and *rotis*. In the south, rice plays a much larger part in people's diets, and fish is important in coastal areas. Another staple is *dhal*, a thick stew made from lentils. However, a common feature of much Indian food is the use of a wide variety of spices, such as cardamom, ginger, saffron, turmeric or coriander, to give endless subtle

◄ These women are making *chapatis* on a simple, wood-burning stove. The *chapati* is a staple part of the diet of northern India.

variations of flavour. Hot green and red chillis are also used in much Indian cooking, giving it a distinctive intensity.

FAMILY LIFE

There is a very strong emphasis on the unity of the family group in India, and the extended family is still strong. Boys will often follow their fathers into the same job or business. In the north and central parts, and particularly in rural areas, women are still restricted in terms of the work they do and the education they may receive. In some traditional Hindu and Muslim families women wear a veil and are kept in seclusion from society – although this is now quite rare. Nevertheless, it is still very common for a bride to be chosen for a young man by his parents, who may advertise for a suitable partner. Once a girl is married, she moves away from home to join her husband's family. However, particularly in urban areas, these traditional ways of life are changing as increasing numbers of women live more independent lives outside the home.

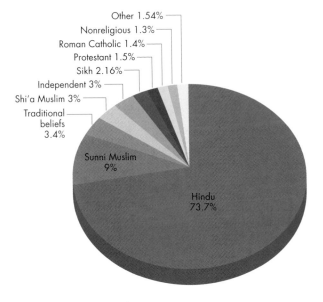

Other 1.54%
Nonreligious 1.3%
Roman Catholic 1.4%
Protestant 1.5%
Sikh 2.16%
Independent 3%
Shi'a Muslim 3%
Traditional beliefs 3.4%
Sunni Muslim 9%
Hindu 73.7%

▲ India's major religions

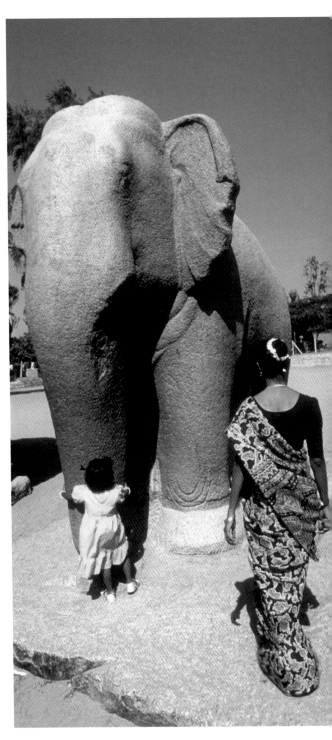

▲ A family visit to the Pancha Rathas, a shrine in Mamallapuram, southern India. The woman is wearing a traditional sari, a long piece of fabric wrapped around the waist and then draped over a blouse and an underskirt.

THE CASTE SYSTEM

The structure of Hindu society is based on an ancient system that originated in one of the Hindu holy books, the *Rig Veda*. According to this scripture, human society is divided into four social classes, or *varnas*: the Brahmins (priests and teachers), Kshatriyas (soldiers and administrators), Vaishyas (merchants and business people) and Shudras (farmers and peasants). All those people who fall outside these classes became known as Untouchables, or later 'Dalits', and they were left to perform tasks that were considered dirty or demeaning such as cleaning, or burying the dead.

This structure of *varnas* later became known as the caste system. In this system, a Hindu is born into a particular *varna* that he or she cannot leave. Although the caste system no longer dictates the type of work a person should follow, it is still a powerful force in Indian society. For example, people from the same caste tend to marry each other. However, any form of discrimination based on caste is now illegal, and in the cities the caste system is becoming less influential as other factors such as education and profession become increasingly important in modern Indian society.

RELIGIONS

Although India is officially a secular country, religion is a central aspect of life for most Indians. Following Partition, Hinduism became the majority faith in India, and today Hindus make up about 80 per cent of the Indian population. Hinduism is unlike most other religions in that it has no founder, no single, central scripture, and no commonly agreed set of teachings. While most Hindus believe in one Supreme God, they worship many deities, and most homes have a room with a small shrine for family members to pray. Hindus worship at dawn and dusk, usually at their home shrines, often by lighting lamps or offering food. Chanting, meditation and *seva*, service to others and to God, are part of a Hindu's religious practices.

Although only just over 12 per cent of Indians are Muslims, because of its huge population India has the third largest Muslim population in the world after Indonesia and Pakistan. In many Indian towns and villages, Hindu temples and Muslim mosques stand side by side.

◀ Indian Muslims offer prayers at the Moti mosque in Bhopal. They are celebrating Eid al-Adha which marks the end of the *hajj* (pilgrimage) to Makkah.

Buddhism (see page 9), Sikhism, Christianity and Jainism are the other main religions in India. Buddhism was once widespread in India, but today it is largely confined to the northeast of the country. Sikhism was founded by Guru Nanak in the Punjab in the late 16th century, and the largest concentration of Sikhs is still to be found in the northwest of the country. Jainism has strong links to both Hinduism and Buddhism, and its present-day form originated in the 500s BC, when a prince called Mahariva taught his followers to consider all living things sacred and to strive for pure lives. Today, India's population of Jains is found mostly in the northwest state of Gujurat. Christianity was brought to India in the early centuries of its history, as well as by missionaries during the colonial period. There is a large Christian community in the state of Kerala.

▲ The prayers on these Hindu prayer flags are printed in Sanskrit.

 Did you know?

Mahatma Gandhi championed the cause of the Untouchables and fought to end discrimination against them. He called them Harijans – 'people of God'.

Focus on: Hindu festivals

India has many religious festivals celebrated at different times and by different parts of the community across the country. The main Hindu festivals include *Diwali* and *Holi*. *Diwali* is the festival of lights and for many Hindus marks the New Year. It lasts for five days in October or November and is celebrated with the lighting of lamps and candles, musical chants and prayers, and with fireworks. *Holi* marks the beginning of spring and is marked with bonfires and processions of music and dancing, during which people playfully throw coloured powders and water at each other.

▲ Indian women throw coloured powder and water during Holi celebrations in Kolkata.

 Did you know?

Hindus believe that bathing at Cape Comorin, where the waters of the Indian Ocean, the Arabian Sea and the Bay of Bengal meet, will wash away their sins. Cleanliness and purity are important aspects of the Hindu religion.

CHAPTER 12

Leisure and Tourism

In India, the dividing line between work and leisure is often not as clear-cut as it is in Western countries, where people typically work from nine to five during the week and relax at the weekends. In many rural areas 'leisure' may not amount to much more than chatting to someone in the market, or while taking a break from working in the fields. In the towns and cities, however, the increase in material wealth and the exposure to a wider range of leisure activities and sports through television are bringing about many changes.

WATCHING TELEVISION

Television itself represents the biggest change in the way in which people spend their time outside work. The national network, Doordarshan, is controlled by the government and before the 1990s provided the only TV channels available for Indian viewers. The introduction of international satellite television and cable in the early 1990s revolutionized Indian television. Those with access to cable television are able to watch foreign channels such as the BBC, CNN news and StarTV, while there are many Indian satellite companies offering a wide variety of programmes including games shows and soap operas.

> **? Did you know?**
>
> The Indian version of 'Who Wants to be a Millionaire?' is the most popular programme on Indian TV. In India it is known as *Kaun Banega Crorepati* which means literally 'Who will become a multi-millionaire?'.

◀ Dramatic make-up and hand gestures are the hallmark of Kathakali dancing, a theatrical artform from Kerala in southern India. Such traditional artforms are under threat from the increased dominance of television in India.

▲ Posters pasted along a street wall advertise the latest Bollywood films.

Focus on: Bollywood

India's film industry is the largest in the world, and Indian films are popular not only at home but also across the world. The industry is known as 'Bollywood' – a corruption of Hollywood and Bombay (now known as Mumbai) where most of the films are produced. Every year 1,000 films are released in India. Bollywood films are often romantic, colourful, 'feel-good' musicals or action-packed adventure films, usually with singing and dancing. India's most popular actor is Shashi Kapoor who has starred in countless movies.

PLAYING SPORT

Cricket and football have been popular in India since they were imported by the British during colonial times. Indeed, Indians are passionate about cricket. During an important match, many people follow the progress of every ball by listening to the radio commentary. A match against India's main rival, Pakistan, arouses particular passion, and on occasions has led to violent clashes between supporters of the two teams. At times of great tension over Kashmir, matches between the two countries have been suspended.

Although not as popular as cricket, field hockey is India's national sport. India dominated the world of hockey in the early days of the

▲ Cricket is the sport of choice in India and is played wherever there is enough open space. Supporting the national team is almost like a religion and can bring cities to a halt.

Olympics, winning all six gold medals between 1928 and 1956. Some traditional games are still hugely popular in India, particularly *kabadi*, a game of tag played between two teams. In 2010, India will host the Commonwealth Games in Delhi, with 71 participating countries in 17 different sports.

TOURISM

India boasts some of the most famous attractions in the world, including the Taj Mahal. In 2006, 4.45 million tourists came to India, 16.5 per cent of whom were from the UK and 15.7 per cent from the United States. Over 8 million Indians take holidays abroad, but increasingly Indians are travelling as tourists in their own country. In 1996 there were 140 million domestic tourist visits but this figure had risen to 461 million by 2006. The potential of the domestic tourist market is only just being realized, and developments such as cheap internal flights (see page 40) are helping to boost this important sector.

Tourism in India

▸ Tourist arrivals, millions: 4.447

▸ Earnings from tourism in US$: 9,227,000,000

▸ Tourism as % foreign earnings: 4.6%

▸ Tourist departures, millions: 8.340

▸ Expenditure on tourism in US$: 9,296,000,000

Source: World Bank

India offers the tourist a very wide range of destinations. The beaches of Kerala and Goa have been popular for some time for a relaxing holiday in the sun. Some tourists visit wildlife parks, hoping to see endangered animals such as tigers and lions, while others make tours of India's extraordinary historic buildings, hill forts, temples and shrines. Eco-tourism, in which the aim is to make as little impact as possible on the local environment as well as benefiting the lives of local people, is also becoming increasingly popular in India, with holidays such as bird-watching, and safaris on offer.

Another form of holiday that has become increasingly popular is the 'yoga holiday'. *Hatha yoga* is a form of physical and mental exercise that has its roots in Hinduism. It is practised widely in the West, and many people come to India to stay in an *ashram* – a religious community – and learn *hatha yoga* in the country in which it originated. Yoga means 'union' in Sanskrit. Many other forms of yoga are part of the Hindu tradition, including meditation and breathing practices that are designed to help a practitioner attain union with God.

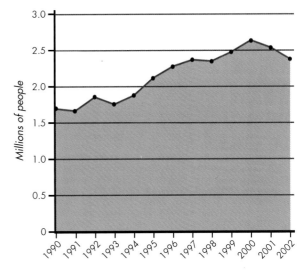

▲ Changes in international tourism, 1990-2002

Focus on: The 'Golden Triangle'

The most popular tourist circuit in India takes in three cities in the north of the country – Delhi, the Mughal city of Agra and Jaipur, the capital of the state of Rajasthan. The tour, known as the 'Golden Triangle', can be covered in a week and also includes the Taj Mahal, the most-visited site in India. However, the Indian government is keen to promote the country's many other lesser-known attractions, for example the fabulous temples of southern India, or the exotic delights of the Thar Desert. Adventure holidays, including Himalayan mountaineering, white-water rafting and trekking, are also being marketed for overseas and domestic tourists.

▲ The Taj Mahal in Agra was built by the Mughal emperor Shah Jahan as a tomb for his favourite wife.

CHAPTER 13

Environment and Conservation

I ndia has an extraordinary variety of landscapes, plants and animals, including Indian elephants and some of the world's most endangered species, such as the Bengal tiger and the Ganges river dolphin. But the country's expanding population and its headlong dash to industrialize have put ever-increasing pressure on its delicate ecosystems.

ENVIRONMENT AND THE GOVERNMENT

In 1984 there was a gas leak at the partly US-owned Union Carbide chemical plant in Bhopal, in central India. More than 3,000 people died and thousands more were seriously injured by the poisonous gas. This incident raised awareness of environmental and safety issues in

Focus on: Project Tiger

Around 1900 it was estimated that there were 40,000 tigers in India, but by 1972 there were only 1,827 left. A national ban on tiger hunting was imposed and Project Tiger was set up. By 2002 the tiger population stood at 3,642. There are now 27 Project Tiger reserves covering nearly 38,000 sq km (14,700 sq miles) of the country. However, India's tigers are still threatened by poachers, and from people such as miners who want to exploit

the land. There is also a problem with local communities who live near or on the edges of reserves, and who see the tigers as a threat to both themselves and their livelihoods. It is vital for the future survival of the tigers that local people are consulted more carefully about decisions that affect them, and that those who have to co-exist with the tigers receive benefits from tiger conservation, such as income from tourism.

◀ Two Bengal tigers take a swim in one of India's national parks. The tiger is a protected animal in India.

industry, and led to the creation of a new department in the Indian government, the Ministry of Environment and Forests (MoEF). The MoEF took charge of all areas of conservation and protection of wildlife and the environment, as well as pollution-monitoring and control. Nevertheless, policies to promote the country's economy have usually taken preference over environmental policies, and India faces some major environmental problems.

AIR POLLUTION

Together with water pollution (see page 44), air pollution is one of the most serious environmental problems in India, causing thousands of deaths every year. Urban areas such as Delhi, Mumbai and Kolkata are some of the most polluted cities in the world. The pollution is the result of increased traffic emissions as well as industrial activity. Measures to curb this pollution have been introduced but are often not effectively enforced. Diesel-powered vehicles, which cause high levels of air pollution, are now banned from the centre of Delhi and all buses

are being converted from diesel to compressed natural gas. In Bangalore, motorists turn off their engines whilst waiting at traffic lights to reduce pollution.

India's rapid industrialization has also had a major impact on its carbon dioxide (CO_2)

▲ A motorcyclist wears a scarf for protection against traffic fumes near the Chandi Chowk bazaar in Delhi.

Environmental and conservation data

▱ Forested area as % total land area: 8%
▱ Protected area as % total land area: 4.9%
▱ Number of protected areas: 539

SPECIES DIVERSITY

Category	Known species	Threatened species
Mammals	390	88
Breeding birds	458	72
Reptiles	521	25
Amphibians	231	3
Fish	5,749	9
Plants	18,664	244

Source: World Resources Institute

emissions. CO_2 is given off when fossil fuels such as oil, coal and natural gas are burned, and is a major factor in global warming. In 2004, India had the fifth highest levels of CO_2 emissions in the world, with 4.6 per cent of the global total. This amount is still low compared to the United States (20.9 per cent) or China (17.3 per cent). However, as the world's most rapidly expanding economies, growth in emissions from both China and India is expected to outstrip that of other countries. Bringing India's CO_2 emissions under control, while continuing to allow the country to develop economically, is vital as part of the international strategy to tackle global warming.

FARMING ACTIVITIES

It is not always easy to reconcile the activities of farmers with conservation and protection of the environment. Modern farming methods make use of artificial fertilizers and pesticides which contain harmful chemicals that pollute groundwater supplies. And although national parks and wildlife sanctuaries have been designated, farmers often encroach illegally on this land for cultivation. Elephants are also still killed for ivory from their tusks, despite the fact that the world ivory trade has been subject to a ban by the Convention on International Trade in Endangered Species since the early 1990s.

DEFORESTATION

Deforestation is another major environmental issue in India. The felling of trees for both industrial and agricultural use has left soils bare and resulted in severe soil erosion. Without tree roots to anchor the soil, many dams are beginning to silt up, as unprotected soil runs off the surrounding hillsides into reservoirs. Trees absorb CO_2, so the removal of tree cover has also affected the levels of CO_2 in the atmosphere.

WATER RESOURCES

Despite the annual monsoon rains and the floods that they often bring (see page 17), clean water for drinking is a scarce resource in India. Population growth and rapid urbanization have put great pressure on the water supply, and many people in India have to queue every day at communal water taps to pick up their supplies of water. Water is needed for industry and to irrigate land for crop production, but a rapid and unregulated increase in demand in some places has depleted groundwater reserves to dangerous levels, drying up rivers and making soils dry and prone to erosion.

▲ These trees have been felled on the Western Ghats to provide fuel for nearby tea-processing factories.

In the past, most villagers got their water from hand-operated wells, limiting the amount of water that could be drawn in a day and the depth of the well. The introduction of pump-operated wells has allowed water to be obtained more easily, and from deeper wells, sucking underground reserves dry. In urban areas, such as Bangalore, it is estimated that 40 per cent of water is wasted in transportation. While the construction of big dams to create reservoirs to store water has been one solution supported by the government in the past, because of the environmental and social problems associated with big dam projects many people now favour smaller, local projects to address the water crisis. The Integrated Watershed Development Programme is funded by the government and allows communities to construct small dams and other structures to store rainwater and replenish groundwater supplies. The 'integrated' approach of this programme also aims to address other environmental problems such as deforestation and soil erosion that relate to water conservation.

▲ Young children pump water from a well in Uttar Pradesh.

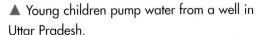

Types of habitat

- Wetlands & water bodies 1%
- Sparse & barren 4%
- Urban 0.2%
- Forest 8%
- Shrubland 18%
- Croplands 68.8%

Focus on: Scrapping ships

Half of the world's ocean-going fleet ends its life on a beach at Alang, in Gujarat state. Here, ships are dismantled and the pieces sold off as scrap. Many of the ships that arrive in Alang could not be broken up in their home countries because of strict environmental laws. The ships are often full of pollutants, such as asbestos, heavy metals and toxic paints, and the local environment is suffering as a result.

CHAPTER 14

Future Challenges

I ndia is a country in the process of very rapid economic and social development. Any country undergoing such changes has to come to terms with their impact, and India is no exception. Traditional customs are being challenged, especially in urban areas where satellite TV, tourism, foreign businesses and shops have brought new ideas and ways of life, particularly for young people.

◀ Television sets are packaged for export in Agra.

INDIA'S POPULATION

One of the most pressing problems for the future is India's population growth. The expansion of the population has already put huge pressure on the environment, on agriculture and on the country's infrastructure – its roads, railways, education and health care. Although many Indians have benefited from the country's breath-taking economic growth since the early 1990s, many millions of people, mainly in rural areas, still live in poverty and struggle with disease and malnutrition. Providing adequate food, health care and education for all, and therefore bridging the gap between the wealthy and the poor, is one of the main challenges for the Indian government for the future.

KEEPING THE PEACE

India's relations with its neighbour Pakistan present another major challenge for the future, particularly as both countries have nuclear weapons. Recent developments have been hopeful, with a meeting between the Indian prime minister Manmohan Singh and the Pakistani president Pervez Musharraf in April 2005 ending in a joint statement from the two leaders stating that peace between the two countries was now 'irreversible'. Although the dispute over Kashmir has yet to be finally resolved, the need for the two countries to work together in the region was starkly highlighted by the aftermath of the earthquake in October

2005 which killed around 50,000 people. India will also have to keep the peace within its borders, between its Hindu and Muslim populations. Although the BJP is no longer in power, the Hindu majority has a powerful voice in the country, and the balance between different communities needs to be carefully maintained.

▲ A group of young children play and wash in the slum district of Mumbai. Hundreds of thousands of children live in these conditions all over the city, and improving the quality of their life is one of the major challenges for India in the future.

LOOK TO THE FUTURE

Many times in its past, India has accommodated and absorbed different cultures, and it prides itself on the assimilative nature of its society. Despite the problems it faces, there are many reasons to be optimistic about India's future. The key to its future development lies in its people and its economy. Many Indians who would once have emigrated to countries such as the United States are now choosing to stay at home to work in India's thriving economy. Although India suffers from low levels of literacy amongst the poor, it nevertheless has an excellent university system producing well-trained graduates who have helped to fuel its economic growth. India is a fast-developing country which is set to become a major player on the world stage.

Timeline

c. 3500 BC Settlement starts in the fertile valley of the Indus river.

c. 2500 BC Indus Valley civilization reaches its peak.

c. 1700 BC Indus Valley civilization declines.

c. 1500 BC Aryans from central Asia begin to move south into India.

c. 1500-1200 BC Hindu texts, the *Vedas*, written.

c. 500 BC Buddhism founded in India.

530 BC Persians invade India.

326 BC Greeks, led by Alexander the Great, invade India.

321-184 BC Period of Mauryan Empire.

272-232 BC Rule of Mauryan emperor, Asoka.

320- c. 500 AD Period of Gupta Empire.

700s Muslims reach India.

1192 Muslim armies conquer much of northern India and establish Delhi Sultanate (1206).

1398 Sack of Delhi by Mongol leader, Timur.

1498 Portuguese sailor Vasco da Gama lands at Calicut in India.

c. 1500 Sikh religion founded by Guru Nanak.

1526 Babur founds the Mughal Empire.

1857 Indian uprising against British rule.

1858 End of Mughal Empire. British government takes over rule of India from the East India Company.

1885 Indian National Congress Party founded.

1914-18 Indian troops fight in World War I.

1919 Massacre in Amritsar.

1920 Mahatma Gandhi starts civil disobedience campaign against the British.

1930 Mahatma Gandhi leads Salt March.

1947 (15 August) India becomes independent. Jawaharlal Nehru is India's first prime minister. Thousands of people die after Partition.

1948 Mahatma Gandhi assassinated. War with Pakistan over Kashmir.

1965 Second war with Pakistan over Kashmir.

1966 Indira Gandhi becomes prime minister.

1971 War with Pakistan; East Pakistan becomes Bangladesh.

1975 Indira Gandhi declares state of emergency (until 1977).

1984 Indian troops storm Sikh Golden Temple at Amritsar. Indira Gandhi assassinated. Bhopal gas leak kills more than 3,000 people.

1991 Rajiv Ganghi assassinated.

1992 Demolition of Babri mosque at Ayodhya leads to widespread violence between Hindus and Muslims.

2001 Earthquake in Gujarat kills at least 30,000 people.

2002 More than 800 people die in religious violence between Hindus and Muslims.

2003 Ceasefire agreed in Kashmir.

2004 India starts to withdraw troops from Kashmir. Manmohan Singh becomes first Sikh to be India's prime minister. Tsunami kills thousands on India's east coast.

2005 Floods and landslides kill more than 1,000 people in Mumbai and Maharashtra. An earthquake kills thousands of people in Kashmir.

Glossary

Alluvial Describes clay and silt deposited by slow-moving rivers. Alluvial soils are usually very fertile.

Aryans People originally from central Asia who moved south into India around 1500 BC.

Biotechnology The study and use of living microorganisms in industrial processes.

Buddhism A world religion that started about 2,500 years ago. The founder of Buddhism was Siddhartha Gautama (c. 563-c. 483 BC), who became known as the Buddha – the 'enlightened one'.

Cash crops Crops that are grown to be sold.

Caste system In Indian Hindu society, the system by which a person's place in society is determined at birth.

Colony A territory that is ruled by another country.

Compensation Money paid as reparation for a loss or an injury.

Constitution An agreed set of rules and laws.

Deforestation The clearance of trees from land that was once covered by forest.

Deity A god.

Democracy A political system in which representatives are chosen by the people in free elections.

Dowry Money or property brought by a woman to a marriage, or money paid by the groom to a bride or her parents.

Dravidians The local people of India before the arrival of the Aryans.

Dynasty A series of rulers from the same family who succeed one another in power.

Ecosystems The relationships between living things and their surrounding environments.

Ethnic Describes a way of grouping people according to shared customs, beliefs and often language.

Federal Describes a way of organizing a country in which power is shared between the central government and regional governments.

Fossil fuels Types of energy sources, such as oil, coal and gas, that are formed by fossilized plants and animals. They release carbon dioxide when they are burned.

Genetically modified Describes plants or other organisms in which the genes have been deliberately altered or moved in order to improve the organism in some way.

Hindi The official language of India (with English), one of the family of Indo-European languages.

Hindu Describes a follower of Hinduism, a native religion of India. Hindus worship many gods and goddesses and believe that a person is reborn many times into many different lives.

Hybrid An animal or plant that is the result of cross-breeding between different species.

Hydroelectric power The production of electricity by harnessing the power of moving water.

Industrialization The process of developing factories and manufacturing on a large scale.

Malnutrition Deficiency in the nutrients that are essential for the development and maintenance of the body.

Monsoon The seasonal winds that are generated by the difference in air temperatures over the Asian landmass and the sea, which bring regular rainfall to the Indian subcontinent.

Mosque A Muslim place of worship.

Muslim A follower of the religion of Islam.

Nationalist Describes a person or movement with a strong commitment to the culture and interests of their own country.

Partition The term given to the division of India into separate parts at independence.

Republic A country that has a president rather than a king or queen as its head of state.

Sanskrit The ancient language of India, language of the Hindu sacred texts the *Vedas*.

Secular Non-religious.

Sikh A follower of the religion founded by Guru Nanak in the Punjab in the late 16th century that combines elements of both Hindu and Muslim beliefs.

Socialist A supporter of socialism, an economic system in which means of production such as land and factories are owned by the state, rather than by private individuals.

Subcontinent A large landmass that forms a separate, distinct part of a continent.

Subsidies Money paid by a government or other body to help a particular group of people.

Subsistence farming Describes farming in which crops are grown to provide food for the farmer and his or her dependents, with little or nothing left over to sell for cash.

Tariffs Taxes on imports.

Tsunami A giant wave caused by an undersea earthquake.

Urbanization The movement of people from rural areas to towns and cities.

Further Information

BOOKS TO READ

A River Journey: The Ganges
Rob Bowden
(Wayland, 2007)

India (Eyewitness Guides)
Manini Chatterjee, Anita Roy
(Dorling Kindersley, 2008)

The Changing Face of India
David Cumming
(Wayland, 2004)

Nations of the World: India
Anita Dalal
(Raintree, 2004)

Flashpoints: Indian Subcontinent
Anita Ganeri
(Watts, 2004)

USEFUL WEBSITES

http://indiaimage.nic.in/
Gateway to government of India information
on the Web.

http://news.bbc.co.uk/1/hi/world/south_asia/
country_profiles/1154019.stm
BBC site with country profile and links to the
latest news from India.

http://www.cia.gov/library/publications/the-
world-factbook/geos/in.html
The CIA World Factbook gives up-to-date
facts and figures for India.

http://goidirectory.nic.in/
Directory of Indian government websites.

http://projecttiger.nic.in/
Website for Project Tiger.

http://www.ashanet.org/info.html
Website about education for underprivileged
children in India.

Index

About the Authors

Ali Brownlie Bojang is a former teacher of humanities and an education officer for Oxfam. She has written a number of books for young people as well as course materials for teachers.

Nicola Barber is the author of many non-fiction children's books, specialising in geography, history and the arts.